THE ESSENTIAL ACCOUNTING

DICTIONARY

of

KEY FINANCIAL TERMS

by

Linda Jane Hodgson

HOW TO USE
THIS DICTIONARY

This dictionary is intended to assist students in passing A level Accounting and the GNVQ Advanced Business Financial Units. It may also be used by students of related Business and Management programmes and by any Non-Accounting students.

To help you test your knowledge, multiple choice test questions have been set with answers in the appendix.

It is suggested that:

1. You try out the test and work out your score.
   If you score 70% or over, congratulations – you have passed – you probably only need to use the dictionary as reference material.

   If you score less than 70% it is probably because you do not know the meaning of some of the financial terms. It is suggested that you go through the papers and underline the terms you do not know, then look them up in the dictionary and learn them. Try the test again and your score will improve.

2. In the months before your examinations try reading and learning a page of financial terms a day or a week.

3. Another good way of testing yourself is to cover up the terms and read only the definitions trying to think of the term that is meant.

4. Of course you may also cover over the definitions, and try to define the terms yourself – but this may be harder.

5. Finally, close the dictionary and try and write down as many terms and definitions as you can remember.

   Good luck!

TERMS	MEANINGS
Absorption Costing	A method of costing which uses both the direct and indirect costs of a product added together and a percentage for profit to find the price of an item. It is linked to cost plus pricing. Also known as full costing.
Accounting	The recording by a business of its financial transactions (book keeping), the presentation of that information in various report forms and predictions, analysis and decisions that are undertaken in connection with that information. There are several branches of Accounting, the main ones being: **Financial Accounting** - the branch of Accounting dealing with past financial transactions and involved particularly with the preparation of annual financial statements for business including the profit and loss account and balance sheet. **Cost Accounting** - the branch of Accounting dealing with the analysis, control and forecasting of costs. **Management Accounting** - the branch of Accounting looking at financial decision making and analysis within a business.
Accounting Bases	The various methods that have been developed for putting basic accounting ideas into practice, eg the different methods available for depreciating fixed assets such as straight line method and reducing balance method.

Accounting Concepts	The basic ideas or standards which are used in the practice of accounting. Four fundamental ideas are laid down by Statement of Standard Accounting Practice 2 (SSAP2) and they are the ideas of 'going concern', 'prudence', 'accruals' and 'consistency'. There are many others such as 'materiality' which are considered of importance.
Accounting Equation	The relationship between assets, liabilities and capital is an equation and may be expressed as: Assets = Liabilities + Capital. A change in one item will have an equal and opposite change in another.
Accounting Policies	The particular policy or method which a business might choose to follow in preparing its accounts, for instance it might adopt the straight line method of depreciating its assets.
Accounting Rate of Return	A method of Capital Investment Appraisal which looks at profitability rather than speed of return. The formula is:

$$\frac{\text{Average annual profit}}{\text{Average investment}} \times 100$$

	Only costs and income flowing from the investment should be included in the calculation. It is a more comprehensive method than payback but ignores the time value of money.
Accounting Records	The actual books or ledgers in which a business will record its financial transactions. There are four main ledgers:
	Cash Book - into which all cash transactions are entered.

Sales Ledger - where all non-cash sales are entered.

Purchases Ledger - where all non-cash purchases are entered.

General or Nominal Ledger - where all other transactions are entered.

Accounting System	The process of recording information from original documents such as invoices into the accounting records, checking that it has been recorded correctly and then presenting the information in a way which enables the owners and managers of the business to review its progress.
Accounts	May be used to mean the individual accounts into which double-entry book-keeping entries are made eg. rent account, sales account. May also refer to the annual financial statements of a business eg profit and loss account.
Accrual	An expense which is due to be paid during an accounting period but which has not yet been paid.
Accrual Concept	The basic accounting idea or standard that expenses should be matched to the period in which they are incurred rather than the period in which they are paid. Also known as the matching concept.

Acid Test Ratio	A ratio used in the monitoring of the performance of a business and also called the quick ratio or liquid capital ratio. It measures the solvency or liquidity of a business by the following formula:

$$\frac{\text{Current Assets minus stock}}{\text{Current liabilities}}$$

A ratio of 1:1 is expected for a solvent business

ACA   Qualified member of the Institute of Chartered Accountants.

ACCA   Qualified member of the Chartered Association of Certified Accountants.

ACMA   Qualified member of the Chartered Institute of Management Accountants.

Added Value   When a business invests money and resources into a product which can then be sold for profit.

Administration Costs   The costs of running a business which include secretarial and office charges

$$\frac{\text{Administration costs}}{\text{Sales}} = \text{Administration Cost \%}$$

This indicates business performance.

Aged Creditor Schedule   A list of all the debts a business owes to its creditors showing what is owed to whom and when they are due. This is necessary for the management or owners of a business to know so that debts are paid but not before time because it will help the cash flow or money cycle of a business to have money left in it.

Aged Debtor Schedule	A list of all the customers or debtors of a business who still owe money to the business showing how much is owed by which customers and when the money is due. This form of monitoring is called Credit Control and is essential for a business to chase up customers' debts regularly so as to help the money cycle or flow of cash through the business.
Allocation	The process of placing overhead expenses into various categories by virtue of where the cost has occurred and charging the overhead to a particular cost centre or cost unit.
Amortisation	The process of a lease losing value over a period of time.
Annual Report	Companies are required by law in the UK to produce an Annual Report. This contains a Profit and Loss Statement and a Balance Sheet, Notes to the Accounts, the Director's Report, Auditor's Report, Chairman's Statement, Fund's Flow Statement and a Statistical Section.
Apportionment	Dividing up the general overhead expenses between the various departments using the most appropriate basis, eg floor area for dividing up rental expenses.
Appreciation	The increase in value of a fixed asset over a period of time eg Land.
Appropriation Account	Appropriation Accounts appear in Partnership and Company Accounts. In Partnership Accounts the Appropriation Account will show interest on any drawings as an addition to profit or as a credit entry and will show interest on capital and

salaries as a deduction from profit or as a
debit entry. The remaining balance will
then be shared as profits as provided by
the Partnership agreement.
In Company Accounts the Appropriation
Account is used to show tax on profits,
dividends and transfers to reserves.

Assets

Everything the business owns which may
be quantified in money terms and may be
divided into:

Fixed Assets - long term items (with a life
of over a year) owned and bought for use
in the business but not intended for resale
eg. vehicles, machinery and property. Such
assets are tangible and may be seen and
touched. Fixed Assets also includes
intangible assets such as goodwill and
patents which are non-physical.

Current Assets - short term items owned
by a business which may change in value
in less than a year eg. stocks of goods,
debtors and cash and bank balances.

Total Net Assets - fixed plus current assets
less current liabilities.

Assets/Sales Ratio

A business performance indicator.

$$\frac{\text{Sales}}{\text{Net Assets}} = \text{value of sales generated by £1 of assets}$$

AAT

Association of Accounting Technicians.

Audit

A system of making an independent check
on accounting figures and accounts.
Auditors may be employed internally by
an organisation to place checks on
accounting figures prepared. However
company accounts must be checked or
audited by an independent firm of

professional accountants. The auditors must check that the accounts give "a true and fair view" of the affairs of the company. This is an annual requirement and is to protect the interests of shareholders.

Auditors	The professional accountants who carry out the checks on company and other accounts and accounting figures and make a report accordingly.
AVCO	A method of Stock Valuation which uses weighted average cost. This is found by dividing the total purchase price of units by the number of units. This figure is then used to value closing stock.
BACS	Bankers Automated Clearing System. A computer system used by the Banks which allows for electronic transfer of amounts between Bank Accounts. No cheque needs to be written but the system requires a remittance advice to be sent from the payer to the payee advising that the BACS transfer has been made.
Bad Debts	If a debt cannot be paid to a business by a customer the debt becomes bad. This may occur if the customer becomes bankrupt, dies or goes missing. The business is allowed to charge the Bad Debt as an expense in its end of year profit and loss statement thus reducing its profits. Good credit control reduces bad debts.
Bad and Doubtful Debts Provision	An amount written off to the profit and loss account to cover debts that may become bad or doubtful in the future. This amount is either shown as a deduction from Debtors or included as a separate Liability in the Balance Sheet.

Balance Sheet

The balance sheet of a business gives a snapshot of the financial position of the business at a particular date. It is based on the Accounting Equation that:

Assets minus Liabilities = Capital

It is one of the main financial statements of a business and is usually prepared at yearly intervals based on the accounting records of a business.

Assets - everything the business owns expressed in money terms, including fixed assets (property, machinery, vehicles etc) and current assets (stock, debtors, cash and bank balances).

Liabilities - everything the business owes expressed in money terms including short term liabilities (Bank overdraft and Creditors etc) and long term liabilities (Long term loans).

Capital - the money invested into a business by its owners.

Balancing Off Accounts

To find how much balance exists in any account in double entry bookkeeping, it is necessary to add up both sides and to insert the difference on the smaller side to make it equal the larger side. This closing balance will then be carried down to the Trial Balance and will be the opening balance on the account for the following period.

Bank Giro Credit

If a business wishes to pay a bill by means of cheque directly to a Bank account it may pay over the counter of a Bank or Post Office by filling in Bank Giro Credit slip. This saves having to post the cheque and is a more secure and efficient way of paying by cheque.

Bank Statement	The Bank's account of all payments in and out of a Bank Account will be sent to the Business at regular intervals in the form of a Bank Statement. The Statement will show:
	Account Details - name, branch and address of Bank, name and number of account.
	Transaction Details - date of each transaction, particulars of each transaction (eg cheque, direct debit), amount paid in or withdrawn, balance at a particular date.
	CR - credit, money in the account.
	DR - debit, overdraft.

Bank Reconciliation Statement	A statement drawn up by a business to ensure that the balances shown in the Bank Statement and the business Cash Book agree.

Blanket Absorption Rate	In absorbing of overhead costs it is usual to calculate separate absorption rates for separate departments. However as a simplification it is possible to calculate one overall absorption rate known as a blanket absorption rate.

$$\text{eg} \quad \frac{\text{Total overheads} \quad £30,000}{\text{Direct Labour Hours} \quad 10,000} = £3$$

Book-keeping	The recording of business transactions is known as book-keeping. Single-entry book-keeping has been in existence since Egyptian and Roman times.
	The system of Double-entry book keeping was first formulated by Luca Paciolo in Venice in 1494. It is based on the principle that every transaction in business has a twofold effect. Every one transaction must be entered in two separate accounts and the entries must be equal and opposite to

one another. They must be equal in terms of date and amount but opposite in terms of being either a receipt of money or value (a debit) or a giving out of money or value (a credit) The double-entry system enables a balance to be achieved which provides a mechanism (trial balance) for testing the accuracy of the accounts.

| Breakeven Point | The point at which total business sales revenues equal total costs so that neither a profit or loss is made by the business. Breakeven point may be calculated by the formula: |

$$\frac{\text{Total Fixed Costs}}{\text{Contribution (sale price less variable costs)}} = \text{Breakeven point}$$

The breakeven point is often shown by a graph. The breakeven point is where the total sales and the total costs line cross on the chart.

It is vital for a business to calculate its breakeven point so that it may know when a product will start to be profitable. It is also an important part of business planning.

Margin of Safety - is the difference between the breakeven point and the actual level or sales value of production.

Profit or Loss - is the difference between sales revenue and total costs.

| Budget | A budget is a financial plan or forecast for a set period of time often twelve months. Business budgets can be, for example: |

Sales Budgets - the expected sales income for the year.

14

Capital Budgets - the expected expenditure on Capital items such as fixed assets for the year.

Trading Budget - the expected sales income and trading expenses for a year.

Cash Flow Budget - all the expected cash income and expenses (both Capital and trading) for a year.

Budgets are an important part of business planning.

Business	Any organisation involved in a trading activity with a view to achieving profits. A business organisation may be:

Sole Trading - owned and managed by a person individually

Partnership - two or more people acting together in a business jointly owned by them.

Private Company - business having the legal status of a company but having only privately owned shares.

Public Company - a business having the legal status of a company which may be publicly owned.

Business Entity Concept	The rule that business accounts must relate only to the specific business being described. They must not include private financial expenses or income relating to the owners and they must not include the expenses or income of any other business.

Business Performance	The way a business is assessed against other businesses and its own performance for past years by extracting ratios and percentages from key figures in its profit and loss statements and balance sheets. The ratios look at profitability, solvency and general performance of the business.
Business Plan	A plan describing what a business intends to do, who will run it, what its income and costs are expected to be, who its customers are and what its vision is for the future. A Business plan will often need to be presented to a Bank or other provider of finance to show the business can be profitable and will be able to repay any money it borrows.
Buying Procedures	The process of a business buying goods or services from a supplier is known as purchasing. Efficient purchasing is important for a business and has often been described as buying the right quantity and quality at the right time from the right supplier at the right price.
Capacity Variance	A fixed overhead variance which looks at the difference between the capacity available and the capacity used. This is then multiplied by the standard fixed overhead rate per direct labour hour.
Capital	The money invested in a business by its owner or owners which provides finance for the starting and running of the business. Capital is also used to describe the fixed assets of a business such as property, machinery and vehicles.

Capital Account	In partnership cases the capital account shows the amount of long-term resources put into the business by each partner. Usually there is little movement in the account. It only needs to be adjusted if a partner brings in more long-term resources or withdraws some existing capital. The other occasion when it will need adjusting is when an existing partner retires or a new partner is admitted.
Capital Allowance	An allowance against profits which is given for tax purposes in respect of expenditure on fixed assets. The allowance is given in place of depreciation.
Capital Budget	The expected expenditure by a business on its fixed assets (premises, machinery, vehicles, equipment etc) and any other Capital items (non-trading) items over a period of time.
Capital Employed	The total of the owner's investment in the business plus any loan and reserves.
Capital Investment Appraisal	Capital investment appraisal is concerned with the type and mix of fixed assets employed by a business and the decision as to which assets to purchase. Because of the importance of making the best long term investment decisions several appraisal methods are used:

Payback - looks at the time it takes for the outflows to be repaid by net cash inflows. **Accounting Rate of Return** - looks at profitability rather than speed of return and takes into account depreciation. |

cont'd...

Discounted Cash Flow (DCF) - looks at the time value of money and reduces future cash inflows to their present day values (Net Present Value).

Internal Rate of Return - is true interest rate earned.

Capital Redemption Reserve	The Companies Act requires that when shares are redeemed an equal amount is transferred from revenue reserves to a Capital Redemption Reserve. This is to maintain the Capital of the Company.
Capitalisation	When certain costs are treated as additional assets of the business and are included in the Balance Sheet rather than being written off to the Profit and Loss Account as expenses.
Cash	The most liquid of all the Current Assets of a Business being the amount held in notes and coins by a Business at a particular point in time and being the balance in the Business Cash Book.
	The constant flow of cash around a business is vital to its continued existence and is the lifeblood of any business.
	The amount of cash held by a business at a particular date is a current asset and will appear in the Balance Sheet as such.
Cash Book	The Cash Book is one of the Books of Original Entry in the full Double-entry Bookkeeping system. It is also a Division of the Ledger. The Cash and Bank being the two busiest accounts are allocated a Book of their own known as the Cash Book into which all Cash transactions are entered.

Cash Budget	A Cash Budget or a Cash Flow Budget is an attempt by Management to ensure that the business does not run into liquidity problems in the future. It is often calculated on a monthly prediction basis and shows Cash receipts, Cash payments and monthly balances and ongoing balances. Expenses of a non-cash nature such as bad debts or depreciation are excluded. Also Capital cash receipts and expenses are included so balances are not the same as profits. It is a test of liquidity rather than profitability and will forecast whether borrowing will be required or whether there will be surplus cash balances.
Cash Flow	The flow of cash around a business is also known as the money cycle. This may be expressed as a Cash Flow Forecast of predicted cash balances based on estimated cash inflows and outflows over a given period of time. A Cash Flow Statement, by contrast, is produced at the end of an Accounting period showing the actual movement of cash in and out of a business during a given period.

Cash in flows - will come into the business from Capital invested, loans and sales of goods or services to customers.

Cash out flows - will go out from the business in the form of purchases to suppliers and trading expenses. Purchase of fixed assets will also cause a cash outflow.

Timing - the timing of cash flowing in and out of a business is vital. A balance needs to be obtained so that money out does not run ahead of money coming in.

Cash Flow Forecast	A cash flow forecast is used to predict the cash coming in and going out from a business over a period of time and at weekly or monthly intervals to ensure that a balance will be achieved.
Cash Residue or Surplus	If a business is trading profitably the amount of cash income will exceed the cash expenses which over a period of time will create a cash residue or surplus left over.
Cheque	A written order to a Bank signed by its customer (known as the drawer) to pay a specified amount to a specified person (known as the payee).
	Cheques are often used in business by buyers of goods and services when settling bills by post.
Cheque Guarantee Card	Where a cheque is being given personally it is usual to ask for sight of a cheque guarantee card whereby the Bank will guarantee payment up to a certain amount.
Club Accounts	Non trading and non profit making institutions such as clubs and societies tend to keep single entry accounts and at the end of the year prepare a Receipts and Payments Account. This needs to be converted to an Income and Expenditure Account to conform to Accountancy standards. Because a club is non profit making, an excess of income over expenditure is known as a surplus not a profit.
Company Accounts	Company Accounts differ from those of sole traders and Partnerships in that they are controlled by the Companies Acts. Companies enjoy a separate legal entity which is distinct from the entity of the

owners who are protected by limited liability. Companies are required by law to produce accounts and to submit them annually to Companies House. Companies are owned by the shareholders or members and are run by the Directors who may or may not be shareholders.

Computers and Accounting

Originally all bookkeeping and accounting was performed by hand. More recently much of the work is done with the aid of computers. This has not affected the principles of Double-Entry Book keeping however and it is necessary for computer operators still to understand double entry. Computers do however enable larger accounts to be maintained and speed up the process of accounting.

Conservatism

Also known as Prudence. This is an Accounting concept that provides that losses should be anticipated in accounting but that gains and profits should never be.

Consistency Concept

An accounting requirement that once a policy for a particular item in the accounts has been adopted the same policy should be used from one period to the next. Any change in policy must be justified and disclosed in the accounts.

Contingency Liability

A business liability that is dependent on the outcome of some future event.

Continuous or Rolling Budget

A method by which a budget may be continuously revised so that it is updated to take account of market or economic changes.

Contra Entry	Sometimes one business might both purchase from and sell to another business. In such cases money may not change hands or not for the full amount. The transaction has to be recorded by a contra entry or set off to preserve accounting and Double-entry principles.
Contract and Job Costing	This is the process of keeping separate cost records for each individual job when the job is unique or for each separate contract. This is in contrast to process costing which is used where jobs are not individual but where there is mass production and a continuously flowing production process.
Contribution	The difference between the selling price of an item and its variable costs. This difference will make a contribution to meeting the fixed costs.
Contribution pricing	Also known as marginal cost pricing is a way of pricing special sales to take up any under-used capacity in a business. Often the prices are lower than normal prices but as long as the selling price is higher than the variable costs the additional sales will make a contribution to meeting the fixed costs or to profits. An example is an airline selling spare seats on an aircraft at lower prices.
Control Accounts	Although not strictly part of the double-entry bookkeeping system, control accounts are a very useful tool. In the Sales Ledger and Purchases Ledger separate records are kept for each Debtor and Creditor. The Control Accounts will summarise and check these entries and may be kept in the General Ledger. They are also a very useful tool in Incomplete

Records cases where the Sales and Purchases figures may have to be reconstructed from the Control Accounts.

Corporation tax	Tax paid by companies and calculated on Company profits.

Correction of Errors

Because of the large number of transactions that will go through the books of a business, errors will occur some of which will be picked up through the Trial Balance, although others may not be. The main categories of errors are:

Errors not picked up by the Trial Balance:

Error of Omission - A transaction completely left out of the books.

Error of Commission - A purchase or sale is entered in the account of the wrong creditor or debtor

Error of Principle - A entry is entered in completely the wrong category of account
Error of Original Entry - A wrong amount is entered into the books.

Errors that will be picked up by the trial balance:

Error of transposition - only a single entry is made, two entries are made on the same side or the two amounts entered on opposite sides are different. This is often dealt with by creating a Suspense Account to force the Trial Balance to balance.

Costs

The expenses incurred by a business in buying or producing goods or services for sale. Costs may be divided into:

Capital costs - buying fixed assets such as vehicles or machinery for use in the business.

cont'd...

Trading costs - the trading expenses of selling the goods or services such as rent, wages, insurance.

Trading costs may be further subdivided into:

Direct or Variable costs - costs which are directly related to and vary with amount of sales, such as purchases.

Indirect or Fixed costs - which do not vary directly in relation to amount of sales such as rent.

Cost Concept	This is the practice of showing assets at cost in the Balance Sheet. This is known as the historic cost and has the benefits of being a simple and objective system. It has the disadvantage of leaving out assets that have no cost for example goodwill. Also it does not recognise that assets may increase in value especially in times of inflation and does not always lead to a realistic financial picture.
Cost Volume Profit Analysis	Another term for break-even analysis. A break even chart will show the point at which business revenue exactly equals total business costs and no profit or loss will be made. It also shows the relationship between fixed costs, variable costs and revenue at all levels of output to enable analysis and decisions to be made. Hence it is also known as Cost Volume Profit Analysis or CVP.
Costing	The way in which business costs are calculated so that they may be taken into account when decisions are taken on how to price goods and services.

Several methods are possible. The main methods are:

Absorption Costing - the method whereby all costs relating to an item (both variable and fixed costs and both direst and indirect) are used and thus absorbed to make a pricing decision.

Marginal Costing - the method whereby only the variable or direct costs are included when making a pricing decision.

Standard Costing - the method whereby an estimated cost is calculated in advance and used in pricing and a comparison is later made to establish any difference between the standard and actual costs once these are known.

Cost of Goods Sold	Those direct costs (usually raw materials, labour and production overheads) which can be related directly to the goods sold. When deducted from Sales in the Trading Account they provide a calculation of Gross Profit.
Cost Plus Pricing	A method of calculating price by taking into account the total costs of goods or services and then adding a margin for profit (this margin may be calculated as a mark up on costs or as a profit percentage).
Credit	1. Buying or selling goods or services when payment is made at a later date. 2. In Double-entry book-keeping a credit entry is made in the business books when money or value leaves the business.
Credit Card	A card enabling a holder to buy goods or services up to a certain amount. The amount spent is then owed to the Credit Card Company and interest will be due if it

is not paid within a certain date. The Business from whom the goods or services are purchased will receive its money directly from the Credit Card company.

Credit Control	The process whereby a business keeps a record of what is owed by customers and sends reminders for what is owed and taking such action as is necessary such as Solicitors letters and Court Action Effective credit control will help the cash flow of a business.
Credit Note	A 'refund document' which is issued to the buyer by the seller when unwanted goods have been returned usually because they have been damaged or are faulty. No money has yet changed hands so the Credit Note will reduce what is already owed by the buyer or reduce the cost of future purchases.
Creditors	A person or organisation which is owed money. Often in Business these will be the Trade Creditors who are Suppliers owed money by the business for goods or services supplied.
Current Account	In partnership cases the current account shows the amount of short-term funds contributed by each partner. The double entry is made between the appropriation account and the current account.
	Interest on Capital, salary and profit share are debited to the appropriation account and credited to the current account of the particular partner.
	Drawings and interest on drawings are debited to the current account of each partner and credited to the appropriation account.

Current Asset	A business asset, which, if it is not already in cash form is expected to be converted into cash by the business within twelve months of the Balance Sheet date. The usual Current Business Assets are Stock, Debtors, Cash at Bank and Cash in Hand.
Current Liability	An amount owed by the Business which will have to be repaid by it within twelve months of the Balance Sheet date. The usual Current Business Liabilities are Creditors and Bank Overdraft.
Current Ratio	A ratio used to test the solvency or liquidity of a Business (its ability to pay its own current debts) by comparing the Current Assets with the Current Liabilities as shown by its Balance Sheet.

Method:

$$\frac{\text{Current Assets}}{\text{Current Liabilities}}$$

A ratio of 2:1 is expected for a solvent business.

Day Books	In book-keeping financial transactions are entered initially into day books or journals or cash books before being posted to an account in the ledger.

An example of a day book is a purchases day book where individual purchases from suppliers are listed on a daily basis. The entry in the ledger (the first stage in the double entry process) can then be made at periodic intervals.
i.e. debit purchases account
      credit suppliers accounts

Debentures	Long term loans usually secured on a company's assets and appearing in the Balance Sheet.

Debit	In Double-entry book-keeping the receipt into a business of money or value is a debit.
Debit Card	A plastic card issued to its customer by a Bank or Building Society which enables the customer to buy goods or services by paying by direct electronic transfer of the funds within the customer's Bank or Building Society Account. No Cheque needs to be written. Common forms of such cards are *Connect* or *Switch*.
Debt	A sum not yet paid by a customer who has been sold goods on credit terms (by paying later).
Debt Factoring	A method of selling off Business Debts to a Factor or Agent in return for a percentage of the total value of the debts. The Factor will then manage and collect the total debts.
Debtors	Amounts due from customers who have bought goods or services from a business but have not yet paid. Debtors are a Current Asset.
Debtors Collection Period	This analysis shows how long, on average, debtors (customers who have not yet paid) take to pay for the goods bought by them on credit. The formula is:

$$\frac{\text{Debtors}}{\text{Sales for the Year}} \times 365 = \text{debtors collection period}$$

30 days may be considered acceptable.

Delivery Note	A Delivery Note is sent with the goods by the Supplier to the Purchaser. It gives precise details of the goods ordered and being delivered.

Depreciation

The amount a fixed asset is expected to lose in value during its life in the business (whether through use, the passage of time obsolescence through technology or market changes).

The term is defined precisely by SSAP 12. The calculation can be made by various methods:

1. Straight line method

In this method the asset is deemed to lose value by an equal amount each year. Example:

$$\frac{\text{Cost of Asset - scrap value}}{\text{Number of years of life}} = \text{Annual Depreciation}$$

2. Reducing balance method

In this method the asset is deemed to lose the greatest amount of its vaue in the early years of its life. Example:

Year 1   Cost of asset x (say) 20% = depreciation
Year 2   Depreciated or reduced value of asset
          x (say) 20% = depreciation

3. Revaluation method

This method is usually applied to assets which are so small it is not worth making the calculations at 1 or 2 above. Example:

Tools cost £100, now worth £80 = depreciation £20.

Differential Costs

Financial accounting uses original or historic costs. When it comes to future decisions however historic costs are irrelevant and the accountant is seeking to ascertain avoidable future costs. Costs which stay the same whichever decision is taken are irrelevant but the costs which will differ with different decisions are the relevant ones and these are known as Differential costs.

Direct Debit	When a business is allowed to collect money from someone else's Bank Account by the BACS system this is known as a Direct Debit. It is a very useful system for the payment of regular bills, eg Mortgage payments.
Direct Costs	Costs that relate directly to the production of goods or services eg raw materials. They may also be known as marginal or variable costs.
Directors	Directors are appointed by a company to control the day to day running of the business for which they may be paid a salary. Together they form a Board of Directors and a Directors' Report is required to be included in the Company's Annual Report.
Directors' Report	The Directors' Report is an essential part of the Company's Annual Report.
Discounted Cash Flow	A Method of Capital Investment Appraisal or Investment Analysis which reduces the value of future cash inflows from a project to their present day expected values by using an appropriate discount factor. The method recognises the time value of money.
Distribution Overhead	These include expenses such as warehouse costs, packaging, transport and depreciation of delivery vans i.e. the costs of distributing the products to the customer.

Distribution of Added Value

Once a Business has completed a trading cycle it may have surplus cash or profit to distribute or share out. This may be done in several ways:

profit to the owners - drawings or dividends;
profit retained or reinvested in the business;
taxation to the Government;
repayment of loans;
financial costs eg interest;
wages and salaries to staff;
payment of any outstanding bills.

Dividends

The share of profits received by company shareholders on their investments is known as dividends.

Dividend Cover

The relationship between the amount of profit reported for the year and the amount distributed as dividends.

Dividend Yield

The relationship between the amount of dividend per share and the market share price of listed companies.

Double-entry Book-keeping

A system of book-keeping whereby two entries are always made in the business books for every one transaction which takes place. The two entries must always be equal and opposite to one another so that the books will balance. They are equal in amount and date of entry but opposite in that one entry will be:

A debit entry - money or value into the business.

The other entry will be:

A credit entry - money or value going out of the business.

Drawings	The amount withdrawn by a sole trader or partner from a business over an accounting period is known as drawings. It represents the owner's financial reward for running the business at a profit, it represents a withdrawal of Capital and appears in the Capital section of the Balance Sheet.
Earnings	Another word for income or wages in business.
Earnings Per Share	The amount of profits after tax, but before extraordinary items, attributable to shareholders by a business divided by the number of shares issued.
EDI	Electronic Data Interchange. A system whereby purchase orders, invoices and other business documents may be sent directly between the computers of the buyers and sellers. Payment will be made at a later date. It assists businesses in the ordering of stock so that a "just in time" system may be used.
Efficiency Variance	The difference between the standard or expected hours to be worked on a project and the actual hours worked on a project multiplied in each case by the standard wage rate per hour.
Equation	There are two very important Equations used in Accounting:

1. The Accounting Equation:
Assets - Liabilities = Capital

This is the basis behind the double-entry book keeping system and enables all balance sheets to balance. It means that what the business OWNS in assets less what it OWES to other people will always equal its Capital or what has been invested in the business by the OWNERS.

2. The Trading Equation:
Income - Expenses = Profit/Loss

This is the basis behind the profit and loss account and demonstrates that a profit or loss is simply the difference between the trading income or sales of a business and its trading expenses or costs. If the income is greater than the expenses a profit will be made. If expenses are greater than income there will be a loss.

Errors, Correction of

Because of the volume of transactions involved, book keeping is subject to some errors. These fall into various categories.

Errors not picked up by the Trial Balance:

Error of Omission - a transaction is completely left out of the business books

Error of Commission - a purchase is entered in the books of the wrong creditor or a sale is entered in the books of the wrong debtor.

Error of Principle - an item is entered in the wrong class of account.

Error of Original Entry - a wrong amount is entered in the business books.

Errors picked up by the Trial Balance:

Error of Transposition - does not conform to Double-entry book keeping principles.

Equity

The amount of money that has been invested in a business by the owners.

Expense	Another word for costs in business the benefit of which is entirely used up in the earning of the revenue to which the cost relates.
Extraordinary Item	A significant amount of income or expenditure arising from events which are outside the ordinary activities of the business and which need to be separately disclosed.
Factor	An agent providing a business financial service eg a Debt Factor.
Finance	1. Money provided for the running of a business. 2. The providing of the money to run a business. Several types of business finance are common: Owners capital or savings; Government grants; Short term Bank overdrafts; Short and long term business loans from banks; Venture capital.
Financial Documents	Every time a business undertakes an activity involving money or its value it should record the activity or transaction by completing a financial record and a financial document. The main financial documents are:

Cheque   Paying-in slip
Purchase order   Invoice
Order received note Credit note
Delivery note   Statement
Goods received note Remittance advice
Petty cash voucher   Receipt

Financial Forecasting	Financial planning for a business which looks ahead to its likely monetary needs and how these may be obtained and paid back from business income. The process starts with the Business plan but continues throughout the business life. A cash-flow forecast is an example and will be needed to obtain finance from lenders.
Financial Providers	Organisations such as Banks who will provide finance or money for businesses.
Financial Statements	At yearly intervals a business will produce its annual Report and Accounts. These will consist of a profit and loss statement and a Balance Sheet. In addition it may produce a summary financial statement which is a less formal document.
Financial Transactions	Every time a business undertakes any activity involving money or its value it is involved in a financial transactions. So many such transactions take place in the course of business that it is vital that all such transactions are recorded either by being written down or entered on a computer record.
	To assist this recording process financial documents have been established eg invoices, receipts.
Finished Goods	In a manufacturing business a type of stock consisting of manufactured goods ready for sale.
Fixed Assets	Long term assets owned by the business and held for use in the business not for sale. Common examples are:
	Land, buildings, machinery, equipment, vehicles, fixtures and fittings.

cont'd...

They should be recorded in separate categories as above and are shown at Cost value in the Balance Sheet less any depreciation.

Fixed Costs	Another term for indirect costs or costs which do not vary with the level of sales or production in a business, eg rent.
Gearing	Gearing may be used as a method of monitoring the performance of a business. It looks at the ratio between the long term debt of a business which is owed back to its lenders and the Capital invested by its owners or its equity. A highly geared business has a larger proportion of external debt and is more risky. A low geared business has a larger proportion of owner's Capital or equity and is safer.
Going Concern Concept	The requirement that an assumption is made that a business will continue in operation in the foreseeable future when accounts are prepared.
Goods Received Note	One of the financial documents used in business and used by the buyer to record the receipt of goods when they have arrived from the supplier. Details are checked against the copy of the purchase order.
Goodwill	Goodwill is a business fixed asset which is intangible, which is non physical and cannot be held or touched. Goodwill represents the reputation that a business has built up and the group of loyal customers it has. Because goodwill has been acquired over a period of time it is

difficult to quantify in money terms. Usually it is not included in a balance sheet for the above reasons and because it contravenes the basic accounting principle of valuing assets at their historic cost. However in partnership cases where a partner is joining a partnership or retiring from it, goodwill has to be quantified either as the value that the partner is paying to join the partnership, or the amount of value he or she is entitled to on retiring.

On the occasion that goodwill is quantified the book-keeping will be:

debit - goodwill account

credit - capital accounts (original partners)

When goodwill is written off:

credit - goodwill account

debit - capital accounts (new partners)

Grant	A method of business finance that involves a gift of money to business usually from a Government source probably given to help regenerate a specific locality or combat unemployment.
Gross Profit	The profit as shown by the business trading account and representing the sales income less the cost of goods sold.
Gross profit rate	A way of monitoring business performance by measuring its profitability. Gross profit is measured as a percentage of sales:

$$\frac{\text{Gross profit}}{\text{Sales}} \times 100 = \text{gross profit rate}$$

A high or increasing rate is usually desired.

Hire Purchase	A source of finance for a business which allows a business to acquire an asset by paying a deposit on it and then paying instalments after which the ownership of the asset will pass to the business.
Historic Cost Convention	The convention that assets are valued at the original cost of acquiring or producing them and not at their present market value.
Income Tax	A tax payable on the income or earnings of individuals and unincorporated businesses and partnerships. It is administered by the Inland Revenue and is a direct tex.
Indirect Costs	Business costs which do not relate directly to the level of sales or production and do not vary in accordance therewith. Also known as fixed costs or overheads.
Insolvency	When a business is unable to pay its current liabilities or debts out of its current assets it is technically insolvent.
Interest	The cost of borrowing money on the commercial market is known as interest. Interest is usually expressed as a percentage of the amount borrowed and may have to be paid on a monthly basis. Interest may also be received by businesses on investments made.
Investment	Placing money in an organisation or business or property with the expectation of receiving the investment back with profits.
Invoice	An important financial document which is sent by the seller to the buyer to request payment for goods or services supplied.

Lease	An agreement by which the business will pay a sum of money either in one sum or by instalments either to the owner of an asset or a finance house for the use of the asset over a specific period of time. The ownership of the asset never passes to the leaseholder. The benefit is that the cost of the Capital item is much less than buying it outright. Buildings may be acquired leasehold as may cars and computer and photocopying equipment.
Leasing	The name of the arrangement under which a lease is obtained by the business from a finance house or the owner of an asset for use of that asset over a specific period of time. The arrangement allows a business to acquire a fixed asset without a large Capital outlay of funds.
Ledger	The name given to the 'Books' in which a business keeps its financial records. The Ledger is often divided into several sections: **Sales Ledger** - records all non-cash sales **Purchases Ledger** - records all non-cash purchases **Cash Book** - records all cash transactions **General Ledger** - records all other transactions

Liability	Amount owed by a business. Liabilities may be divided into:
	Current liabilities - short term liabilities due for repayment within twelve months of the date of the balance sheet eg:
	Creditors Bank Overdraft
	Long term liabilities - where repayment is due more than one year from the date of the Balance Sheet eg:
	Bank Loan Mortgage.
Liquidity	A term used to describe the cash resources of a business and its ability to pay its current debts out of its current assets. Another word for solvency.
Loans	A source of finance for a business. Loans are sums of money borrowed often from a Bank which have to be repaid over a period of time Interest will be charged.
Long-term Liability	An amount which is owed to the business and which is payable more than twelve months after the Balance Sheet date.
Marginal Costing	The incremental cost of producing one extra unit. The marginal cost is often the same as the variable cost.
Margin of Safety	In a breakeven analysis, margin of safety is the difference between the breakeven point and the actual production level. It may be expressed as units or in costs and revenue.

Mark Up	A way of adding an amount of profit to costs in order to calculate prices. It is often expressed as a percentage of costs, eg:
	costs £100 mark up (50%) £50 price £150
Market Led Pricing	A form of pricing which looks at the demand in the market for the product rather than the costs of making it. In case of high demand or a monopoly situation a business may be able to set its own prices. In a competitive market a business will have to take account of the prices of competitive products and price accordingly.
Matching Concept	The accruals concept is also known as the matching concept since an attempt is made to match all revenues attributable to a financial period to all expenses attributable to that period.
Materiality	An accounting concept which regards small items which are not material or significant to the business as being capable of being treated collectively in the Balance Sheet rather than individually.
Money Cycle	Basically a term for the cash flowing round a business and comprising money coming in from sales and capital and money going out on purchases and other expenses.
Money Measurement Concept	The concept that the language of business is money and that all business transactions are expressed in money terms or the value of money. This is why it is difficult to include goodwill because it is not easily measured

in money terms. Also the concept demonstrates the limitations of the accounts since they do not give an indication of the non-monetary aspects of business.

Monitoring	A way of reviewing and analysing the performance of a business over a period of time. Business performance is monitored by making comparisons between different businesses, between different years and with expected targets. The differences or variances are then examined and reasons sought for any large differences arising.
Net Assets	The total assets of a business less the total liabilities as shown by the business Balance Sheet
Net Book Value	The value of the fixed assets of a business after total depreciation has been deducted as shown by the business Balance Sheet
Net Loss	The amount by which the business overheads or indirect expenses exceed the gross profit of business as shown by the Profit and Loss Account. Gross profit - overheads = Net Loss (where overheads exceed gross profit) £100 - £150 = (£50)
Net Profit	The amount by which the business gross profit exceeds the business overheads or indirect expenses as shown by the Profit and Loss Account. Gross Profit - overheads = Net Profit (where gross profit exceeds overheads) £100 - £50 = £50

Net Realisable Value	An amount at which stock may be sold in its present condition after deducting any costs incurred in disposing of it. Stock may be valued at Cost or Net Realisable Value whichever is the lower.
Nominal Value	The face value or a share or other security as opposed to its real value.
Opening Stock	The stock of goods held by a business at the start of a trading period and purchased during a previous trading period.
Order	The document by which goods are purchased from another business and known as a purchase order. Sales are recorded by a Sales order.
Order Received Note	Many businesses will record the receipt of an order by an order received note.
Overheads	Another word for indirect costs or the costs associated with running the business and not directly related to the level of goods or services produced or sold eg. rent, insurance, indirect wages, heating lighting etc.
Paciolo	A Venetian who is credited with the invention of double entry book-keeping to assist the merchants in their trading.
Partnership	A business being owned and run by two or more people.
Paying-in Slip	A business document which is used to pay cash and cheques into a Bank Account.

Petty Cash Voucher	A business document allowing small amounts of cash to be paid to business employees for business expenses and which must be authorised before payment is made.
Prepayment	An expense which is not due to be paid within an accounting period but which has been paid in advance.
Price	The amount charged to the customer by a business for the provision of goods or services as agreed between the buyer and seller enabling the sale to take place.
Price/earnings Ratio	The relationship between the latest reported earnings per share and the market price per share.
Pricing Strategies	The particular policy which a business may employ in determining the price of goods or services. The most common are: **Need to make profit** - cost plus pricing **Prices of competitors** - market led pricing **Under-used capacity** - marginal or contribution pricing.
Prior Year Adjustment	An adjustment made in the current year's accounts which reflects something which should have been adjusted in the prior year's accounts but could not be because it was not accounted for at the time.
Profit	The difference between sales earned by a business in a particular period and the costs relating to the sales.

Profit and Loss Statement	This statement shows the income earned by a business and the expenses of earning it for a particular accounting period.
Provision	An amount charged as an expense in the profit and loss account in respect of any expected loss or liability eg. bad debt provision.
Prudence Concept	The Accounting concept which requires that when preparing accounts for a business, provision should be made for all known or expected losses or liabilities but that gains or profits should never be anticipated.
Purchase Order	The document sent by the buyer to the seller to request the supply of goods or services.
Quick Ratio	Another term for the acid test or comparison between the business liquid assets and its current liabilities.
Realisation Concept	The concept that gains or profits are never anticipated in accounting. They are only taken into account when they have been actually realised. This is in contrast to losses which may be anticipated. The concept is linked to the prudence concept.
Receipt	A document given by the seller to the buyer to confirm that payment has been made for a purchase and which shows the date of purchase and the amount.

Reducing Balance	A method of depreciation of fixed assets which gives the greatest amount of depreciation in the earlier years. Example:
	Year 1 = cost of asset x 20% (say) = depreciation
	Year 2 = reduced balance of asset x 20% (say) = depreciation
Remittance Advice	A document sent by the buyer to the seller to accompany payment for goods and to state that payment is being made and for which goods and services.
Reserves	Surplus of profits or Capital made by a business and retained by it for future use.
Retained Profits	Profits reinvested by the owner as additional capital into the business.
Return on Capital Employed (ROCE)	A profitability ratio which looks at the relationship between sales and capital to evaluate and compare business results.

$$\frac{\text{net profit}}{\text{capital}} \times 100 = \text{return on capital}$$

Revaluation Method	A method of depreciation for small assets that allows the asset to be revalued each year. The depreciation is the difference between the value of the asset at the start and the end of the year.
Revenue	Another word for business income.
Royalties	Payments to the owner of the rights to a product eg the author of a book when sales of the book are made by the business.

Sales	Agreement made between the buyer and the seller for goods and services and the money which changes hands as a result.
	Cash Sales - where money changes hands at the time of the transaction
	Credit Sales - where money is paid later by the buyer.
Sales Order Received Note	When an order for goods is sent by the buyer to the seller it is often recorded by the seller on a Sales order received note.
Security Checks	Measures taken by a business to prevent errors and possible fraud. They may consist of authorised signatories, segregation of duties etc.
Selling Procedures	The procedure used by a business when a sale is made. This may involve:
	Cash sales - when money changes hands at time of sale.
	Credit sales - when money changes hands at a later date.
Semi-variable Costs	A fixed cost where one element may be variable. For instance a telephone bill may be a fixed cost element of rental and a variable element of number of calls made.
Share Capital	The amount of money invested into a business by the shareholders of a Company.
Shareholders Funds	A measure of the shareholder's total interest in the company represented by the total of the share capital plus the reserves.

Share Premium	The surplus over and above nominal value received in consideration for the issue of shares.
Solvency	The ability of a business to pay its current debts out of its current assets. Also known as liquidity.
Solvency Ratios	A way of measuring the ability of a business to pay its debts. The main solvency ratios are Acid Test and Current Ratio.
Standing Costing	A method of setting pre-determined levels of costs and revenues as a target for achievement. Actual costs and revenues are then compared with the budgeted figures and variances are calculated.
Standing Order	An individual direct credit made through the BACS system to another person which is set up by the person sending the money.
Statement of Account	A statement of account is usually sent by the seller to the buyer at the end of the month to show details of transactions that have taken place during the month and what is still owing.
Statement of Standard Accounting Practice (SSAP)	Statements issued by the Accountancy Bodies which describe approved methods of accounting.
Stock	The materials and items which a business holds and which it intends to sell.
Straight Line Depreciation	A method of depreciation where the asset value is spread evenly over its useful life.

Sunk costs	The costs that have been invested in a project by a business and will not be recovered if it is abandoned.
Suspense Account	An account used to force a trial balance to balance by placing any differences in a suspense account. It is a temporary measure only and is to allow for the correction of errors before the final accounts are prepared.
Tax	A government levy that is payable in various forms.
	VAT - Value Added Tax - is administered by Customs and Excise and is an indirect tax levied on sales to the customer which has to be collected by a business and paid over at quarterly intervals.
	Income Tax - a direct tax - levied on the earnings of individuals and the profits of businesses and administered by the Inland Revenue.
	Corporation tax - a direct tax - levied on Company profits and administered by the Inland Revenue.
Trading Account	One of the main financial statements of a business which is prepared at the end of a trading period and shows sales or income less the cost of sales and calculates the gross profit of the business.
Trading Cycle	When a product or service is sold by a business a trading cycle has been established. The product or service has been ordered and supplied and money has changed hands, ideally a profit will result or if expenses exceed income there will be a loss.

Trading Forecast	A statement which predicts the expected sales of a business and the expected expenses for that period.
Trial Balance	A trial balance sets out all the balances of all the double-entry accounts of a business and totals all the debit and credit entries in two different columns which should be equal to one another. It effectively checks the book keeping entries that have been made by the business over a period of time and acts as a starting point for preparation of the final accounts of the business.
Turnover	Business income from sales.
Unit Cost	All the direct and indirect costs of producing one item of production or of a service.
Value Added Tax	An indirect tax administered by the Customs and Excise authorities which is levied by a business on sales to its customers and which must be collected by the business and paid over to the Customs and Excise at quarterly intervals.
Variable Cost	Costs which vary directly in relation to the level of production or sales, also called direct costs.
Variance	The difference between an estimated or budgeted figure and an actual figure. Variances may be favourable - where expenses are within budget - or adverse - where expenses are in excess of budget.
Venture Capital	Funds that are invested in business by speculators in the expectation of receiving high returns in the long term.

Winding Up	The name given to the procedure of closing down a business.
Work in Progress	A form of stock held by a business representing goods which are being processed but are not yet in a finished or saleable state.
Working Capital	The current assets held by a business less the current liabilities, in other words the amount of net liquid assets the business has to fund its business.
Zero Based Budgeting	A form of budgeting for a business that does not look at previous years' budget figures but assumes a base of zero and asks for all budgeted income and expenses to be justified.

MULTIPLE CHOICE TEST

For each question please circle the MOST APPROPRIATE answer.

1 **Which is correct:**
   A Assets + Liabilities = Capital
   B Capital + Assets = Liabilities
   C Assets = Liabilities + Capital
   D Capital = Liabilities + Assets

2 **Double-entry book-keeping involves:**
   A Two entries being made in the business books which are equal and opposite to one another
   B Two sets of books being kept for the business
   C Business book-keeping being kept by more than one person
   D Every entry in the business books being checked twice

3 **A DEBIT in the business books represents:**
   A An asset
   B A payment out
   C A liability
   D Money or value received

4 **Your CREDITORS are:**
   A People who owe you money
   B People who provided the original capital for the business
   C People to whom you owe money
   D Your employees

5 **Which of the following CANNOT be a current business asset:**
   A Bank overdraft
   B Stock
   C Debtors
   D Pre-payments

6 **Which of the following CANNOT be a current liability:**
   A Accruals
   B Creditors
   C Directors' loans
   D Cash

7   A CREDIT entry in the business books represents:
- A   Money or value given
- B   Payment of a debt
- C   Money overdrawn at the bank
- D   Drawings

8   Working capital is:
- A   Total assets less liabilities
- B   Current assets less current liabilities
- C   Capital invested in the business by the owner
- D   Long-term liabilities.

9   Cost of sales represents:
- A   Stock
- B   Total business expenses
- C   Depreciation
- D   Purchases adjusted for stock

10 GROSS profit represents:
- A   Income less direct costs
- B   Income less total costs
- C   Profit before taxation
- D   Turnover

11 NET profit represents:
- A   Profit after taxation
- B   Income less total costs
- C   Income less direct costs
- D   Drawings

12 Which is NOT a ledger account in the books of a business:
- A   General Ledger
- B   Sales Ledger
- C   Purchases Ledger
- D   Discount Ledger

13 Which statement is NOT true:
- A   Cash sales are entered in a Cash Book
- B   Credit sales are entered in a Sales Ledger
- C   Cash purchases are entered in the Purchases Ledger
- D   Credit purchases are entered in the Purchases Ledger

14 DEPRECIATION represents:
A   A decline in business trade
B   Discount to customers
C   A decrease in value of fixed assets
D   An increase in value of fixed assets

15 Which of the following would NOT appear in a Profit and Loss Account:
A   Drawings
B   Depreciation
C   Bad debts
D   Accrued expenses

16 Which of the following would NOT appear in a Balance Sheet:
A   Depreciation
B   Accrued expenses
C   Drawings
D   Overheads

17 Which is NOT true:
A   Owner's capital is increased by net profit
B   Owner's capital is decreased by net loss
C   Owner's capital is decreased by drawings
D   Owner's capital is increased by drawings

18 Equity Capital is:
A   The owner's capital in a business
B   Long-term loans
C   Dividends to shareholders
D   Director's salaries

19 Dividends represent:
A   Bonus payments to employees
B   A payment to shareholders representing a share of the profits
C   Discounts to customers
D   Interest free loans to directors

20 Which is NOT a method to depreciate assets:
A   Straight line method
B   Revaluation method
C   Market value method
D   Reducing balance method

21 All directors are:

A Employees of a company
B Owners of a company
C Customers of a company
D Shareholders of a company

22 All shareholders are:

A Company employees
B Directors of a company
C Owners of a company
D Customers of a company

23 Corporation Tax is payable by a company on:

A Net profits
B Gross Profits
C Turnover
D Directors' fees

24 Income Tax is payable on:

A Directors' fees
B Purchases
C Sales
D Turnover

25 VAT is calculated on:

A Gross profit
B Net profits
C Sales
D Directors' fees

26 A trial balance will NOT detect:

A An arithmetical error
B A transaction for which only one entry is made
C A debit wrongly cast as a credit
D A transaction completely left out of the books

27 Which of the following is NOT an accounting concept or convention:

A Materiality
B Prudence
C Going concern
D Economy

28 Which of the following is NOT a recognised branch of accounting:

A Financial accounting

B Creative accounting

C Cost accounting

D Management accounting

29 A business will make a net loss if:

A Total expenditure exceeds total income

B Total expenditure is lower than income

C Turnover is greater than total costs

D Total costs are less than total income

30 Double-entry book-keeping was an invention of:

A Galileo

B Paciolo

C Sage

D Pythagoras

NOTES

Answers to
MULTIPLE CHOICE TEST

1.	C	16.	D
2.	A	17.	D
3.	D	18.	A
4.	C	19.	B
5.	A	20.	C
6.	D	21.	A
7.	A	22.	C
8.	B	23.	A
9.	D	24.	A
10.	A	25.	C
11.	B	26.	D
12.	D	27.	D
13.	C	28.	B
14.	C	29.	A
15.	A	30.	B.

GREENWICH EXCHANGE BOOKS

Business and Administration

Need to Know series
All paperback unless otherwise stated. (ISBN Prefix 1-871551 applies)

Competition in Local Government by James Hodgson (-03-1)
How to manage competition for local government services - now available on disk only.

Managing Schools by James Hodgson (-01-1)
An introductory guide for those new to devolved school management. Video also available.

Going It Alone by Kevin Wellman (-03-X)
A guide for those looking to start their own service business.

Servicepoint Work Book and Video by Norman Flynn and James Hodgson (-51-X)
For managers and students of service marketing.

The Headteacher: skills for successful leadership by Richard Epps and James Hodgson (-52-8)
This book is aimed at supporting Heads in their role of leading and managing schools.

Student Guides

Greenwich Exchange Student Guides are critical studies of major or contemporary serious writers in English and selected European languages. The series is for the Student, the Teacher and the 'common reader' and are ideal resources for libraries. *The Times Educational Supplement (TES)* praised these books saying "The style of these guides has a pressure of meaning behind it. Students should learn from that .... If art is about selection, perception and taste, then this is it."

(ISBN prefix 1-871551- applies)

The series includes:
W. H. Auden by Stephen Wade (-36-6)
William Blake by Peter Davies (-27-7)
The Bröntes by Peter Davies (-24-2)
Joseph Conrad by Martin Seymour-Smith (-18-8)
William Cowper by Michael Thorn (-25-0)
Charles Dickens by Robert Giddings (-26-9)
John Donne by Sean Haldane (-23-4)
Thomas Hardy by Sean Haldane (-35-1)
Seamus Heaney by Peter Davies (-37-8)
Philip Larkin by Warren Hope (-35-8)
Shakespeare's Poetry by Martin Seymour-Smith (-22-6)

Tobias Smollett by Robert Giddings (-21-8)
Alfred Lord Tennyson by Michael Thorn (-20-X)
W.B. Yeats by Warren Hope (-34-X)

Other titles planned include:
20th Century: T. S. Eliot; Ford Madox Ford; Robert Graves; Dylan Thomas
19th Century: Arnold; Jane Austen; Browning; Byron; John Clare;
S. T. Coleridge; George Eliot; John Keats; Oscar Wilde; Wordsworth
18th Century: Fielding, Dr Johnson; Alexander Pope; Richardson;
Laurence Sterne; Sheridan; Dean Swift
17th Century: Congreve; Dryden; Ben Jonson; Marlowe; Milton; Rochester

Early writings: Chaucer; Skelton

European Languages
Fifty European Novels by Martin Seymour-Smith (-49-8)

French Authors
Balzac by Wendy Mercer (-48-X)

Other titles planned include:

Apollinaire; Céline; Gide; Proust; Rimbaud; Tournier, Verlaine; Zola

German Authors
Goethe; Heine; Thomas Mann; Rilke

OTHER GREENWICH EXCHANGE BOOKS
All paperbacks unless otherwise stated.

LITERATURE & BIOGRAPHY

"The Author, the Book & the Reader" *by Robert Giddings*
This collection of Essays analyses the effects of changing technology and the attendant
commercial pressures on literary styles and subject matter. Authors covered include
Dickens; Smollett; Mark Twain; Dr Johnson; John Le Carré.
ISBN 1-871551-01-0 Size A5 approx; 220pp; illus.

"In Pursuit of Lewis Carroll" *by Raphael Shaberman*
Sherlock Holmes and the author uncover new evidence in their investigations into the
mysterious life and writing of Lewis Carroll. They examine published works by Carroll
that have been overlooked by previous commentators. A newly discovered poem,
almost certainly by Carroll, is published here. Amongst many aspects of Carroll's
highly complex personality, this book explores his relationship with his parents,
numerous child friends, and the formidable Mrs Liddell, mother of the immortal Alice.
ISBN 1-871551-13-7 Size 70% A4; 130pp; illus.

"Norman Cameron" *by Warren Hope*
Cameron's poetry was admired by Auden; celebrated by Dylan Thomas; valued by Robert Graves. He was described by Martin Seymour-Smith as one of "... the most rewarding and pure poets of his generation..." is at last given a full length biography. This eminently sociable man, who had periods of darkness and despair, wrote little poetry by comparison with others of his time, but always of a high and consistent quality - imaginative and profound.
ISBN 1-871551-05-6 A5 size; 250pp; illus.

"The Essential Baudelaire" *by Professor F. W. Leakey*
A chronological survey of Baudelaire's writings this book will offer for the first time in Baudelaire studies, a comprehensive survey of his writings in their full chronological development. Baudelaire's development is explored under five headings: the Verse Poet; the Novelist in Miniature; the prose Poet; the Critic and Aesthetician; the Moralist; the translator. This book will interest Baudelaire specialists as well as the general reader.
ISBN 1-871551-3 A5 size; 300pp; illus.

PHILOSOPHY

"Marx: Justice and Dialectic" *by James Daly*
Department of Scholastic Philosophy, Queens University, Belfast.
James Daly shows the humane basis of Marx's thinking, rather than the imposed "economic materialistic" views of many modem commentators. In particular he refutes the notion that for Marx, justice relates simply to the state of development of society at a particular time. Marx's views about justice and human relationships belong to the continuing traditions of moral thought in Europe.
ISBN 1-871551-28-5 A5 size; 180 pp

"Whitehead's Philosophy" *by Dr T. E. Burke*
Department of Philosophy, University of Reading
Dr Burke explores the main achievements of this philosopher, better known in the U.S. than Britain. Whitehead, often remembered as Russell's tutor and collaborator on *Principia Mathematica,* was one of the few who had a grasp of relativity and its possible implications. His philosophical writings reflect his profound knowledge of mathematics and science. He was responsible for initiating process theology.
ISBN 1-871551-29-3 A5 size; 180pp

POETRY

"Wilderness" *by Martin Seymour-Smith*
This is Seymour-Smith's first publication of his poetry for more than 20 years. This collection of 36 poems is a fearless account of an inner life of love, frustration, guilt, laughter and the celebration of others. Best known to the general public as the author of the controversial and best selling *Hardy* (1994).
ISBN 1-871551-08-0 A5 size; 64pp

Baudelaire: "Les Fleurs du Mal in English Verse" *translated by Professor F. W. Leakey*
Selected poems from *Les Fleurs du Mal* are translated with parallel French texts, are designed to be read with pleasure by readers who have no French, as well as those practised in the French language.
F. W. Leakey is Emeritus Professor of French in the University of London. As a scholar, critic and teacher he has specialised in the work of Baudelaire for 50 years. He has published a number of books on Baudelaire.
ISBN 1-871551-10-2 A5 size 140pp

"Shakespeare's Sonnets" *edited by Martin Seymour-Smith*
This scholarly edition follows the original text of the 1609 Quarto - which, with newly revised notes and introduction by Seymour-Smith – provides an insight with which to judge Shakespeare's artistic intentions.
ISBN 1-871551-38-2 A5 size; 120pp

THEATRE

"Music Hall Warriors: A history of the Variety Artistes Federation" *by Peter Honri*
This is an unique and fascinating history of how vaudeville artistes formed the first effective actor's trade union in 1906 and then battled with the powerful owners of music halls to obtain fairer contracts. The story continues with the VAF dealing with performing rights, radio, and the advent of television. Peter Honri is the fourth generation of a vaudeville family. The book has a foreword by the Right Honourable John Major MP when he was Prime Minister – his father was a founder member of the VAF.
ISBN 1-871551-06-4 A4 size; 140pp; illus.